CONTENTS

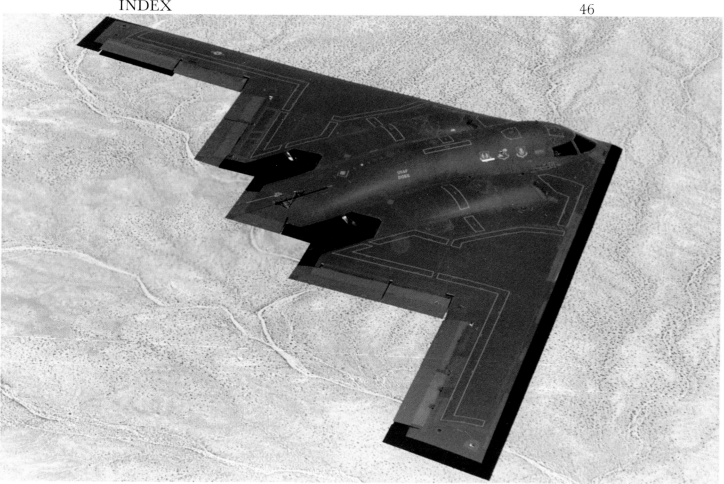

14 August 1980 was a bad day for General Richard H. Ellis, Commander of the United States Air Force's (USAF) Strategic Air Command (SAC). "Today's *Washington Post* story on the possible development of an advanced technology bomber brought the hair up on the back of my neck", he wrote in a memorandum to USAF Chief-of-Staff, General Lew Allen. He demanded that Allen "take immediate action . . . to discredit the story and otherwise defuse the situation".

Reports that the USAF was planning a new bomber had been circulating for more than a week. In its 4 August issue, the trade journal *"Aviation Week & Space Technology"* had reported that the House-Senate Authorization Conference Committee of the US Congress was suggesting not only that a fleet of 100 updated Rockwell B–1 bombers be built for SAC, but that these should be followed by a newer design "using all-new technology, particularly stealth technology to avoid radar detection." A week later, the magazine described the new military aircraft as "the advanced stealth bomber".

Above: In the immediate post-war years, the USAAF (later USAF) continued to rely on piston-engined bombers like the Boeing B-29 and (illustrated) B–50 Superfortress.

"Aviation Week . . . " is not the sort of magazine you can buy on the newsstand. Its circulation is carefully controlled, and largely confined to the aerospace industry (although illicitly-acquired copies are eagerly read within the Soviet intelligence community). What alarmed General Ellis was seeing similar reports appearing in a daily newspaper. "Some Air Force enthusiasts have nicknamed this new bomber 'Stealth' because of its ghost-like qualities", the newspaper claimed. "Technocrats explain that 'Stealth' presents a virtually undetectable 'cross-section' to radar beams searching for it. They call it the High Technology Aircraft."

The decision to develop the new bomber – soon to be labelled the Advanced Technology Bomber (ATB), and later to be designated B–2 – marked the start of yet another attempt by the USAF to develop a replacement

Left: Still reliant on the power of the piston, but boosted by the use of jet power, the B–36 Peacemaker formed Strategic Air Command's (SAC) backbone during the 1950s.

Above: Sleek and swept-winged, the Boeing B–47 Stratojet was powered by six turbojets, the power of which could be augmented by the fitment of Jet-Assisted Take-Off (JATO) units.

for the elderly Boeing B–52 Stratofortress; a long, drawn-out saga of indecision and cancellations which has run for four decades.

BOMBER DEVELOPMENT

From the early days of the Second World War until the early-1960s, the US maintained a resolute policy of bomber development. Even before one generation of long-range bombers had entered service, development of its eventual replacement was authorized. For instance, development of the Boeing B–29 Superfortress was authorized in August 1940, and ordered into production in May 1941, while development of the Convair B–36 Peacemaker commenced in November 1941. This pace was maintained for the post-war subsonic jet bombers: development of the Boeing B–47 Stratojet was ordered in February 1945, followed by the B–52 in summer 1948.

At first, it looked as if this pattern would continue into the supersonic era. In November 1952, Convair was chosen to develop the supersonic B–58 Hustler; while 1955 saw the release of USAF requirements for two long-range supersonic designs able to replace the B–52. These were to be powered by advanced turbojets and a nuclear

powerplant respectively. The nuclear-powered aircraft concept proved short-lived, but the turbojet-powered aircraft emerged as the B–70 Valkyrie, whose development was entrusted to North American Aviation (NAA) in the final month of 1957.

In a world in which ballistic missiles were being rushed into service on land and in nuclear submarines, and with the US being humiliated by a long series of Soviet exploits in space, the new bomber was regarded both by the Eisenhower and Kennedy Administrations as something of an anachronism. In December 1959 the programme was scaled down to cover only a handful of prototypes. August 1960 saw it briefly reinstated as a full development and test programme, only to be returned to prototype-only status in 1961. The first XB–70A prototype

Below: A legend in its own lifetime, the eight-engined B–52 Stratofortress entered USAF service in 1954 – and it's still going strong. Illustrated is a B–52D, complete with two Hound Dog air-to-ground missiles.

Developments And Dreams

create an extensive and effective anti-B–70 defence network.

Firm backing for a force of 50 or even 100 B–70s would have allowed abandonment of the costly and short-lived B–58 Hustler, removed the need for the later General Dynamics FB–111A, and handled the role assigned to the SR–71. It would also have given the US a strike force able to operate with total impunity in the skies above any nation except the Soviet Union throughout the 1970s, 1980s and into the 1990s. Many of the B–52 crews who died over North Vietnam in the *Linebacker II* raids of 1972 would likely be alive today had they been flying B–70s.

Above: Possibly the most grandiose of projects aimed at developing a replacement for the B–52 was North American's huge delta-winged, Mach 3 – capable XB–70 Valkyrie.

conducted its maiden flight on 21 September 1964, the second in July 1965. But less than four years after it took to the air for the first time, the first XB–70A had been permanently grounded and put on display in the USAF museum at Wright-Patterson Air Force Base (AFB), Ohio. The second XB–70A had been lost in a mid-air collision during a routine test flight on 8 June 1966.

SAFETY IN DEVELOPMENT

In retrospect, it is clear that the vulnerability of a Mach 3 aircraft to defensive fighters and missiles had been greatly over-estimated. Neither the Mikoyan-Gurevich MiG–25 Foxbat nor the SA–5 Gammon surface-to-air missile (SAM) were able to intercept the Lockheed SR–71 "Blackbird" throughout that aircraft's long strategic reconnaissance career. Nuclear warheads would have made both weapons more effective, but it is questionable whether the Soviets could actually have afforded to

Above: Though it promised much, the harsh truth was that the XB–70 was not capable of meeting a series of rigorous operational requirements, as defined by the USAF. Defence cuts led to the demise of the project.

Above: On 8 June 1966, during what should have been a routine flight, the death knell for the Valkyrie was sounded when the second XB–70A was lost after a mid-air collision with an F–104 chase-plane.

By the mid-1950s the US and the United Kingdom (UK) were developing the Grumman A2F (A–6) Intruder and Blackburn NA.39 Buccaneer respectively. These subsonic tactical bombers were intended to fly at low level, avoiding engagement with enemy defences by flying under the coverage pattern of long-range surveillance radars. The idea of a low-level strategic bomber was, however, slower to take root. This is hardly surprising given the USAF's experience with its two tactical bomber programmes.

Ordered into development in 1946, the Martin XB–51 proved disappointing. Powered by three General Electric J47 turbojets – two pod-mounted on either side of the forward fuselage and a third installed in the rear fuselage – the aircraft had a short-span, variable-incidence wing. Gross weight at take-off was around 56,000lb (25,424kg). Two prototypes were built, but test flying between 1949 and 1951 showed that the aircraft had a poor radius of action, and a very modest bombload of only 4,000lb (1,816kg).

Developed as a USAF version of the US Navy's Douglas A3D–1 Skywarrior carrier-based bomber, the B–66 Destroyer was intended to serve as a high- or low-altitude tactical bomber, but had a long history of technical problems. It served with Tactical Air Command (TAC) between 1956 and 1963, and some were re-activated in 1967, fitted out as electronic warfare (EW) aircraft and despatched to Vietnam. A few were still in service in the early-1970s.

Except for the B–66 (the jetpowered YB–60 version of the Convair B–36) and the RB–69A derivative of the

Right: Developed as a medium jet bomber, the triple-engined Martin XB–51 was intended to carry up to 10,400lb (4,721kg) of bombs or eight 5in (127mm) rockets in its internal weapons bay.

Lockheed P2V Neptune, all other bomber projects with designations higher than –58 were supersonic. Boeing's proposed XB–59 was a 148,000lb (67,192kg), Mach 2 medium bomber whose shoulder-mounted, swept, short-span wing gave it a distinctive appearance; while Martin's XB–68 looked like a smaller version of the B–58, but with one afterburning J79 under each wing, plus a third inside the aft fuselage. Neither aircraft was built, and all remaining designations between –58 and –70 were subsequently applied to missile systems.

In the early-1960s, the bomber fleets of the USA and the UK were switched to low-level operations. The UK never did develop a dedicated low-level strategic bomber, although the British Aircraft Corporation (BAC) TSR.2 was big enough to have served partly in this role. In the US, however, studies of the first low-level strategic bomber were completed in 1961, well ahead of the first flight of the XB–70A.

LOOKING AHEAD

The Subsonic Low Altitude Bomber was in the weight class of the B–52, and designed to carry a 12,000lb (5,448kg) payload. The follow-on Extended Range Strike Aircraft was in the 600,000lb (272,400kg) class, and had a variable-geometry wing. By 1963 this had been followed by the 360,000lb (163,440kg) Low Altitude Manned Penetrator and the Advanced Manned Precision Strike System (AMPSS).

Developments And Dreams

Left: As the 1960s gave way to the 1970s, so the delta-wing gave way to the swing-wing of the Rockwell B–1A; a bomber haunted by political controversy and double-dealing.

By mid-1965, the AMPSS requirement had been upgraded to include the ability for sustained supersonic flight at high altitude, and to emphasize the need for a reduction in radar cross section (RCS). The new concept was named the Advanced Manned Strategic Aircraft (AMSA). Four years later, this was redesignated B–1A, and a development contract was awarded to Rockwell International in June 1970.

Below: One of the B–1A prototypes, seen here on one of many high-speed, low-level test flights. The ability to fly beneath enemy air defence radars was of paramount importance.

Above: Cancellation of the B–1A by the Carter Administration was to boost development of the so-called "cruise" missile, seen here in its dummy form beneath a B–52 wing.

Above: Designed from the outset to incorporate low-observable RAM technology, Lockheed's futuristic A–12 "black" project represented a quantum leap in RCS reduction.

Production deliveries of the first of 240 Rockwell B–1As should have started in 1979, leading to an initial operating capability (IOC) in 1982; but a change of Administration doomed this plan. In 1977, President Jimmy Carter announced that he would not approve production of the new bomber, but would shift the funding to cover full-scale production of air-launched cruise missiles (ALCM) to arm SAC's B–52 force in the 1980s. Flight tests of the B–1 prototypes would continue, as would development of the aircraft's electronic warfare (EW) system.

SIGHT UNSEEN?

In the next few years, a secret programme codenamed "Sabre Penetrator" studied various advanced bomber con-

cepts based on low-observable technology. While these were going on, a series of bomber penetrativity tests carried out in 1979 at Nellis AFB, Nevada, showed just how well the B–1 could elude modern air defences.

Low-observable technology dates back to the Second World War, when some German U-boats were fitted with schnorkel masts covered with radar-absorbent material (RAM); but it was not until the late-1950s that aircraft and missile designers looked at methods of reducing RCS. Projects from that era which incorporated RCS-reduction measures include the Lockheed A–12 spyplane (from which the SR–71 was derived), the AGM–26B version of the North American Hound Dog stand-off missile, and various Ryan reconnaissance drones.

By the mid-1970s, a decade of secret research had created high-efficiency RAM which could be applied to an airframe on a large scale, plus the advances in computer technology and radar theory needed to control and

Above: Often referred to as first-generation stealth aircraft, the relatively low RCS of the A–12 and SR–71 was somewhat compromised by huge turbojet exhaust plumes.

Developments And Dreams

A 1981 Request for Proposals (RFP) for the Advanced Technology Bomber (ATB) attracted bids from two multi-company teams. The joint Lockheed/Rockwell proposal was based on the former company's expertise gained on the SR–71 and F–117A stealth fighter, and the latter's experience with the XB–70 and B–1A. Boeing, for long the main supplier of bombers to the USAF, opted to team up with Northrop. Work on stealth technology had started at Northrop in the mid-1960s with various small-scale research and development projects, and the company was now ready to exploit this in a production warplane.

Despite Congressional insistence, there was little chance that the proposed stealth bomber could be developed and deployed by the end of 1987. In July 1981 USAF Secretary Verne Orr estimated that a stealth bomber might take up to 10 years to develop, and that this schedule could only be speeded up at what he frankly described as "tremendous cost".

On 2 October 1987, President Ronald Reagan announced that not one but two new bombers would be developed for SAC. To meet the deadline set by Congress, a batch of 100 updated B–1B bombers would be built, while under a separate programme a new stealth bomber could be developed for deployment and front-line service in the early-1990s.

Later that month, Northrop issued a brief 75-word press release:

"LOS ANGELES—Oct. 20, 1981— Mr. Thomas V. Jones, Chairman of the Board of Northrop Corporation, confirmed today that Northrop has been notified by the Air Force of its selection as prime contractor to conduct initial research and development on advanced bomber concepts.

"This effort will have a material impact on Northrop. The key team

predict RCS. In 1976 Lockheed was given a contract to develop several prototypes of the XST, a small aircraft intended to demonstrate suitable technology for a "stealthy" fighter. Flight trials started in November 1977, and led to a 1981 order for the definitive Lockheed F–117A stealth fighter. News of the XST and F–117A soon leaked, but the appearance of the aircraft remained highly classified until November 1988.

In early-1981, Congress decided that a new bomber should be developed for SAC. It made no attempt to dictate what sort of aircraft this would be, but insisted that it enter service in 1987. To launch the programme, $300 million was added to the 1981 Defence Budget to get development started, plus $75 million for long-lead procurement of components whose manufacture would have to begin well ahead of work on the airframe itself.

The USAF was given a deadline of 15 March 1981 to choose its new

Above: In contrast to the gentle curves of the A–12/SR–71, the Lockheed F–117A stealth fighter embraces the sharp, angular lines characteristic of "faceting".

bomber. Within SAC, the favoured solution was the FB–111H, a stretched derivative of the FB–111A powered by two of the General Electric F101 engines developed for the B–1B. By backing a relatively inexpensive aircraft which could be deployed as an interim bomber, SAC hoped that development of an advanced stealth bomber could be carried out on an unhurried timescale. Another faction within the USAF saw a developed B–1 as the best solution, a view shared by many politicians who believed that President Carter had allowed US defences to become weakened during his Administration. Restored to production status, the Rockwell International bomber could be in front-line service by 1986.

members are Boeing, LTV/Vought and General Electric Aircraft Engine Group.

"All details are classified, and no further comments will be made."

The initial development contract was worth $7,300 million. The B–2 represented a significant technical risk, but President Reagan's two-stage bomber deployment programme made this fact acceptable. Even at the high-rate of production planned for the fleet of 100 B–1B, it would be the mid-1980s before the USAF had to decide whether to rely on the B–2, or

Below: Funded, cancelled, then funded again to the tune of 100 production aircraft, the B–1B has an RCS significantly lower than that of the B–52, but is plagued by several technological shortfalls.

to abandon the newer aircraft in favour of buying more B–1Bs or the proposed B–1C – an aircraft with additional stealth features. The first five years of the B–2 programme could thus be used as a technology-demonstration phase.

"From the outset, we stressed that the B–2 is on the leading edge of technology, and there were some very significant technical risks associated with the B–2", USAF Chief-of-Staff General Larry D. Welch was to recall in 1988. "We had some twelve risk areas we identified, and insisted on closure of each of those risk areas before we embarked on full-scale development. Since we closed out that risk reduction effort, we really haven't had any surprises. Since that time, development has proceeded quite smoothly."

Like the F–117A, the B–2 would be a "black" programme – one whose classification would make it near-invisible and virtually immune from Congressional oversight. The first US "black" programme was probably the *Manhattan* Project, which developed the atomic bomb. Signals Intelligence and codebreaking are similarly protected to the present day, while the early-1960s saw the cloak of total secrecy descend on the world of reconnaissance satellites, and the 1970s saw stealth technology similarly classified.

TALKING SHAPE

As was the case with the F–117A, the shape of the new bomber would remain under wraps for as long as possible. Finally, in 1985, Senate Armed Services Committee Chairman Barry

Developments And Dreams

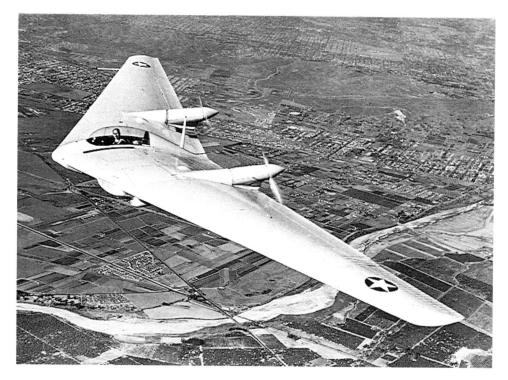

Above: If it was built today, many would describe the configuration of the Northrop N–9M as futuristic; yet this proof-of-concept "flying wing" took to the skies for the first time nearly 40 years ago.

Goldwater revealed that the B–2 would be a "flying wing", a configuration which Northrop had first evaluated in the 1940s.

Northrop's first flying wing had been the experimental N–1M. Flown in 1939, this had impressed the US Army Air Force (USAAF) which commissioned studies of a 250mph (402km/h) flying wing bomber in May 1941. A contract signed in October 1941 ordered a single XB–35, plus the N–9M one-third scale demonstrator. Three more N–9Ms were ordered in 1942, along with a second XB–35.

Maiden flight of the first N–9M was on 27 December 1942. The 7,100lb (3,223kg) single-seat aircraft had a wingspan of 60ft (18.20m) and was powered by two 275hp Menasco C654 piston engines. Unfortunately, the first N–9M crashed on 19 May 1943 after managing only 22 hours of flying time in 44 sorties. The engines had proved troublesome and prone to failure, so the final prototype (designated N–9MB) was fitted with 300hp Franklin O–540–5 engines.

As a result of experience gained with these scaled-down aircraft, it became obvious that the full-sized XB–35 would be deficient in both range and speed. The first XB–35 should have been delivered to the USAF in 1943, but this date slipped because of a shortage of trained engineers at Northrop, and modifications to the design itself. The company was now under contract to build six B–35s after the single XB–35, and in early-1945 was ordered to equip two of these with jet engines.

By now, a jet-powered flying wing was also under test in Germany. Designed by Reimar and Walter Horten, the Gotha Go 229A single-seat fighter had been preceded by an engineless Horten Ho IX VI prototype. Powered by two 1,962llb (891kg) Junkers Jumo 004B turbojets, the Go 229A was 54ft 11¾in (16.66m) in span, and weighed in at 16,550lb (7,514kg) loaded. First flown in February 1945, it had demonstrated a top speed of 497mph (800km/h) during trials the following month, before crashing as the result of a failure of the starboard engine. Gothaer Waggonfabrik completed another prototype, but this had yet to fly when the factory was captured by US troops during the final stages of the Second World War.

TESTING TROUBLES

Northrop finally flew the first XB–35 on 25 June 1946. The aircraft had a wing span of 172ft (52.1m) and was powered by four Pratt & Whitney Wasp Major engines driving three-bladed, contra-rotating propellers mounted at the trailing-edge of the wing. These proved prone to gearbox and propeller problems, and the first prototype was grounded less than three months after its first flight. A second XB–35 flown a year later managed only eight flights and a total of 12 flying hours.

Modified to receive single-rotation propellers and simpler gearboxes, the first aircraft resumed flight test in February 1948. Bad vibration problems were noted, and it soon became obvious that the flying wing configuration was less stable than a conventional design – an undesirable feature in an aircraft intended to drop bombs accurately. Plans were drawn up late in 1948 to re-engine the YB–35 models then under construction with six Allison J35-A–17 jet engines, but even this scheme was dropped in the following year. Some airframes were diverted to the B–49 programme, but most were simply broken up for scrap.

showed that the aircraft was inherently unstable, and that it was near-impossible to hold a steady course, or constant airspeed and altitude. Cancellation was announced on 15 March 1950 — the day a nose gear failure wrecked the aircraft.

By now, the third and final flying wing was on flight test. Another reworked YB–35, the prototype YRB–49A reconnaissance bomber was powered by six 5,600lb (2,542kg) Allison J35–A–19 turbojets. Four were mounted within the wing, the remaining two in external pods: an arrangement which freed space within the wing for more external fuel.

Even before the YRB–49A could fly, the programme was cancelled, the USAF having realized that the aircraft would be out-performed by the B–52. Nevertheless, the aircraft was completed and flown as a research and development exercise, taking to the air for the first time on 4 May 1949. Test flying continued until late-1950, and the aircraft was scrapped in 1953.

Conversion of two YB–35s into YB–49s involved the installation of eight 4,000lb (1,816kg) thrust Allison J–35–A–15 jet engines, plus vertical stabilizing fins and wing fences. The first example flew on 21 October 1947, the second on 13 January 1948. Just after being handed over to the USAF in the summer, the latter aircraft suffered an in-flight structural failure while flying a high-speed, low-level pass which created a high load factor. A low-altitude gust caused the wing to break on both sides, outboard of the engines. The aircraft crashed, killing the crew.

END OF THE LINE

Wind tunnel tests, and an eyewitness account of the aircraft tumbling before impact, made the USAF doubt the stability of the flying wing concept. Further tests with the first prototype

Above: Looking back to the future as one of the astonishing XB–35s shadows a B–17 Flying Fortress, its configuration all the more dated by the former's appearance.

Below: With company confidence in the "flying wing" configuration growing, evermore ambitious plans emerged, including a six-engined concept for transport purposes.

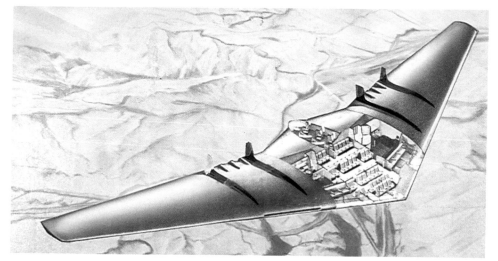

URING the early-1980s, North-rop's sprawling Hawthorn, California, plant was heavily involved in assembly of the F–5E Tiger II and sections of the F/A–18 Hornet. To create a suitable facility for large-scale "black" work, the company purchased a disused Ford Motor Co. auto-assembly plant in Pico Rivera, California, turning this into what was probably the largest secret defence industrial site in the United States. Security was tight, although in May 1987 the *Los Angeles Times* was to claim that several years before, an employee had sneaked up onto the roof of the plant and painted "a vulgar Russian expression that was large enough to be detected by Soviet spy satellites passing overhead".

When specifications for what was then the ATB were drawn up in the late-1970s, the aircraft was designed to be an approximate match for the Soviet Tu–26 Backfire strategic bomber. Designed to cruise at Mach 0.8 over ranges of up to 5,755 miles (9,260km) – a distance equal to the Soviet aircraft's

range – it weighed 280,000lb (127,120 kg) at take-off, and could carry a pay-load of 10,000lb (4,540kg), At an early stage, the design was scaled up several times until it was in the same general range and payload class as the B–1B.

It was also assumed that stealth would allow the aircraft to fly at high altitude throughout its operational life. In 1981, the USAF decided that an ability to fly low-level penetration missions was also required. This required major design

Above: A large but comparitively anonymous car manufacturing plant, the ex-Ford facility at Pico Rivera, Ca., was to get a new lease of life courtesy of the new bomber project.

changes, with obvious penalties in both cost and timescale. SAC could have ordered that the existing wing be strengthened, and accept the risk that further beefing up might be needed at a later stage of the aircraft's career, but chose instead to order a redesign which would cost more and create greater delays, but would improve long-term capability and growth potential. During this work, the configuration of the wing leading- and trailing-edges was revised. By 1986, a full-scale engineering mock-up had been built at Pico Rivera. This allowed the basic design to be frozen, with the last significant additions and modifications being incorporated during that year.

Left: Artistic impressions always come a poor second to the real thing, but to have instantly dismissed this rendering as pure science-fiction would have been a big mistake.

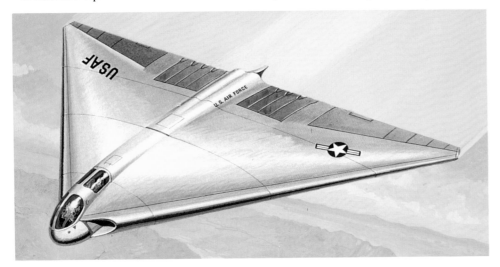

Between the early-1980s and the first flight in 1989, more than 550,000 hours of testing were carried out. This included 24,000 hours of wind tunnel trials of the proposed configuration, 16,000 hours of simulator work to check out the control laws, and 6,000 hours of flight-control system testing using a full-scale test facility. A test rig at Boeing's Seattle, Washington, plant was used to verify the fuel system and landing gear, while another at Northrop tested the environmental control system. An avionics integration laboratory was set up to work on the aircraft's electronic systems.

Other programmes tested mechanical properties of the aircraft's all-composite, load-bearing structure. A wing section was tested to destruction, failing at 1.8 per cent of its design load. Other work assessed the effect of battle damage to the composite structure, and explored the technology needed to repair the airframe in a manner which would preserve its low RCS characteristics.

Much effort was devoted to the highly-specialized research needed to ensure that the bomber's stealth capability would be as predicted. Lockheed's F-117A had relied on a technique known as "faceting" – the use of flat-panels which would deflect rather than reflect radar energy – but this approach produced high aerodynamic drag, an unacceptable feature in a long-range bomber. For the B-2, Northrop would make extensive use of a composite structure either containing RAM or possibly even built from newly-developed radar-absorbent structures (RAS), devising a shape which, if built with great accuracy, would reflect little of the radar energy.

Right: As the "black" bomber project took shape, so tantalizing rumours began to emerge, resulting in a new round of "kite-flying". Note the lack of vertical surfaces on this concept.

HIDE-AND-SEEK

To assess the design's low-observable qualities, RCS measurements were made of scaled-down and full-sized components of the aircraft, and of scaled-down models of the complete aircraft. The latter may have included a half-scale or third-scale flying prototype powered by four non-after-burning F404 engines. This could have been used to prove the flying characteristics of the proposed planform (a wise move given the history of the XB-35 and YB-49) and allowed low-observability trials.

First reports of such an aircraft emerged in the late-1980s, and alleged a first-flight date in 1982. In 1988 one source had claimed that a scaled-down aircraft had been flying for about 15 months, raising the possibility that a rebuild in the mid-1980s had converted the aircraft to a configuration closer to that of the production bomber.

Creation of the B-2 and its associated production facilities required several new or improved technologies. The airframe includes heavy-laminate structures; tape-laminated, integrally-stiffened structures and large contoured surfaces; large composite channel sections; and long, constant-section parts created by a continuous process which forms and partially cures the end product, allowing it to be cut off at the correct size.

When designing the F-117A, Lockheed used conventional aluminium-based alloys, then applied layers of

ATB: A Vision of the Future?

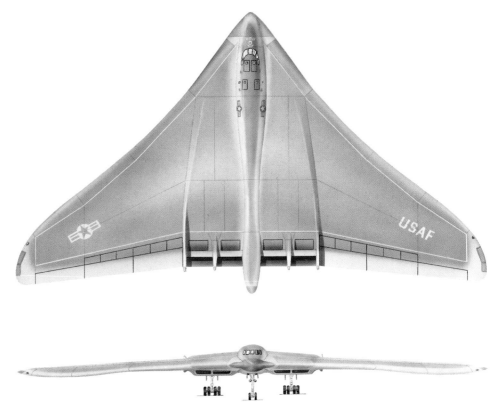

A Wing And A Prayer

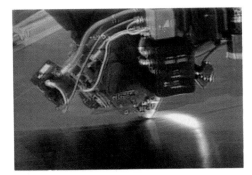

Above: Numerous manufacturing techniques that could be applied to B–2 composite materials were a direct result of an intensive R&D programme initiated during the early-1980s.

external RAM. On the B–2, however, most of the structure is made from composites, and much of the surface is skinned in honeycomb-type RAS material supplied by Hexcel Corporation's Advanced Products Division.

Problems were experienced in manufacturing composite sandwich structures, in which composites are mated to one or more layers of metal, then working these using automated machinery. Typical of the latter is an adaptive drilling machine which uses a microprocessor to detect the changing forces as the drill bit passes from one material to the other in a two or even three-material stack, and adjusts the speed accordingly.

This technique is particularly useful on complex components. Drilling time for each hold on one part made from a layer of graphite, then titanium, then aluminium, was reduced from five minutes to 80 seconds, whilst avoiding the creation of unsatisfactory elongated holes, a problem experienced during early attempts to work on B–2 complex-curved panels. By spring 1989, Northrop had purchased more than 30 adaptive drills; while Boeing was training staff to use the new unit, and pondering its suitability for use on commercial aircraft.

Robotic equipment is used to spray "special coatings" onto substrate materials. The nature of these coatings has not been revealed, but the USAF has stated that their application to the specified standard would have been impossible without the new machines. New technology has also been applied to metal components on the aircraft, as B–2 production involves the machining of complex shapes in aluminium and titanium at higher-than-before metal removal rates, and the accurate and fast machining of small aluminium and magnesium parts.

MEETING THE NEEDS

In all, some 900 new materials and processes had to be developed. These included exotic methods of cleaning the composite components using corona-discharge and ion-gas dusting techniques. Inspection of the aircraft also needed new technology such as real-time radiography, ultrasonic through-transmission, plus film and laser shearography for the testing of honeycomb cores and bonds respectively. The latter technique uses laser interferometry to measure the deflection which occurs when a part is placed under mechanical stress.

Above: Without the extensive use of advanced computer technology, the chances of an aircraft as complex as the B–2 becoming a reality would have been all but impossible.

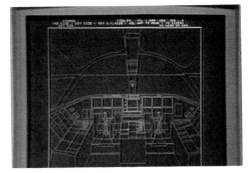

Above: This Northrop Computer-Aided Design (CAD) screen shows one of the cockpit configurations evaluated for possible adoption to house the B–2s two-man crew.

Northrop has spent more than $1 billion of its own money on techniques intended to save money during production, while smaller but still sizeable investments have been made by the other main contractors. One result of this has been a three-dimensional computer graphics system available to Northrop, the main subcontractors and the USAF. At Northrop's Pico Rivera plant alone, there are 30 computer graphics rooms containing a total of more than 400 computer terminals.

This database contains a detailed description of the aircraft which shows not only major sub-assemblies such as panels, pipework and electrical cabling, but which continues down to the level of individual fasteners and other small fittings. It allows design staff to examine any part of the aircraft in three-dimensional detail, verifying fit and clearances. In the past, this kind of work has traditionally been done using a mock-up.

All design and manufacturing staff thus have access to a common agreed source of design data. All changes made are immediately available to all, eliminating the traditional risk that expensive parts might be manufactured to obsolete drawings. Data held in the computer can be annotated with manufacturing instructions, then supplied directly to numerically-controlled machine tools. The computer database thus eliminates drawings, mockups, prototype tooling and prototype aircraft.

Installation of cabling and pipework within a first prototype is particularly difficult, with technicians struggling to make such components conform to the actual shape of the aircraft's innards. Lengths and curvatures are inevitably slightly different to those predicted on the drawing board. Using the computer, however, an electrical cable can be drawn in its planned location, then electronically "unrolled" to determine the correct length which the shop floor must manufacture.

The savings have proved very real. Northrop claims that first-time-fit errors on the B–2 have been reduced by a factor of six, while the reworking of pipework and electrical harnesses fell to only a few per cent. There may, however, still have been some problem areas. Unofficial comments before the rollout from various industry sources claimed that several problems had emerged with electrical cabling and the wing leading-edges.

Developing this advanced computer-aided-design technology was not easy. In 1989, General Bernard P. Randolph, Commander of Air Force Systems Command (AFSC) admitted to *"Aviation Week . . . "* that the computer system has caused "growing pains" during development of the B–2, but stated that these were far outweighed by the benefits. "We would never have been able to pull the B–2 off without computer-aided design."

WHO DOES WHAT

Manufacture of the B–2 airframe is split between three companies. Northrop builds the centre section, including the cockpit, and is responsible for final assembly and systems integration. LTV Aircraft Products Group tackles the fuselage centre section, including the areas which contain the engines and the landing gear. The aft centre section and outboard wings are built by Boeing Advanced Systems. Much of the fuel is carried in this area, and in spring 1990, the US Government's General Accounting Office (GAO) reported that Boeing was having problems in meeting Northrop's specifications when sealing the fuel tanks.

Some compromises were made when building Air Vehicle No. 1 (AV–1). To enhance internal access for servicing, some panels and hatches were made easier to work with, while various test probes and other fittings were installed for use on early flights. Most prominent of these was the trailing air-data probe mounted in a metal tower on the aft fuselage. This was used to calibrate the flush-port system. Surface smoothness was also left to a lower standard for initial flights, but would be improved before beginning low-observable tests. On AV–1, the undercarriage was made from modified Boeing 757/767 landing gear components, but later aircraft will have a custom-designed assembly.

During development, the bomber project remained "black", and no technical information was released. When publishing cost estimates in June 1986, Defence Secretary Caspar Weinberger had warned the press that:

Below: Released on 20 April 1988 to a media hungry for any information on the B–2, this artwork would prove to be quite accurate. Military security demanded that the depiction gave no real detail of the engine exhausts.

A Wing And A Prayer

"We remain thoroughly committed to protecting any and all information that would aid the Soviet countermeasures effort. Accordingly, we think it would be very much against the national interest to make public additional information or data about the aircraft. It would aid the Soviets and no one else."

In May 1987, Congressmen Les Aspin and Samuel S. Stratton proposed that the Pentagon open up production of the stealth bomber to competition rather than assign the contract to a single defence company. However, a study of second-sourcing carried out later that year by the Rand Corporation concluded that the small number of aircraft invovled, plus the high classification of the programme, did not warrant the establishment of a second production line.

The veil of secrecy finally began to rise in early 1988. On 26 January, the USAF announced that on 19 November of the previous year it had awarded Northrop a $2,000 million production contract for the B–2. It also confirmed

that production funding would be provided to the main subcontractors – Boeing, LTV and General Electric – but declined to identify their exact roles in the programme. Nor would the USAF comment on reports that the projected date of the B–2's first flight had slipped. Target date for the rollout and maiden flight remained highly classified.

FUTURE VISION

On 20 April 1988, the USAF released on artist's impression of the B–2. Although this did not show the aircraft's exhausts, it was generally

Right: For such a major project, the public debut of AV–1 was a quite austere and subdued affair. The media and assembled dignitaries were kept well back from the aircraft itself, thus maintaining its mystery.

accurate. "The first flight of the Advanced Technology Bomber, or B–2, is currently scheduled for this Fall", the service announced.

This time-schedule proved over-optimistic, for back at Palmdale, California, things were not going smoothly. In August 1987, a USAF Lockheed C–5 Galaxy transporter had delivered the first set of B–2 wings to Northrop's new final-assembly facility at Palmdale Airport, allowing AV–1 to gradually take shape. Some sub-assemblies seem to have been shipped to Palmdale before all testing had been completed, resulting in unplanned modification work on the newly-assembled aircraft.

"Ship One is literally crawling with people", an unidentified observer told

"Aviation Week . . . " in April 1988, "and most of them aren't Northrop people, because they can't even get on the airplane". The prototype had not yet received its engines, reported the magazine, and a "major redesign of the inlet and powerplant mounting structure" was likely, and could be implemented on the fourth full-scale development (FSD) aircraft. Problems were also reported with the aircraft's windscreen – part of the load-bearing structure – and with cracking of the composite wing leading-edges.

LIFTING THE VEIL

AV–1 was finally rolled out at Palmdale on 22 November 1988. Security was strict, and the small

invited audience was allowed only a frontal view of the aircraft. The rear end – and those mysterious exhausts – were to be kept secret. That at least was the idea; but during the ceremony an overflight by a camera-equipped Cessna 172 light aircraft allowed *"Aviation Week . . . "* to publish unauthorized views of the hidden rear section and the aircraft's novel exhausts, plus vertical photos showing the bomber's exact planform. The wraps were well and truly off one of the best-kept secrets in aviation history.

Below: In all its majesty and glory, the mighty and mysterious new bomber had made its presence felt without even leaving the ground. But would it live up to expectations?

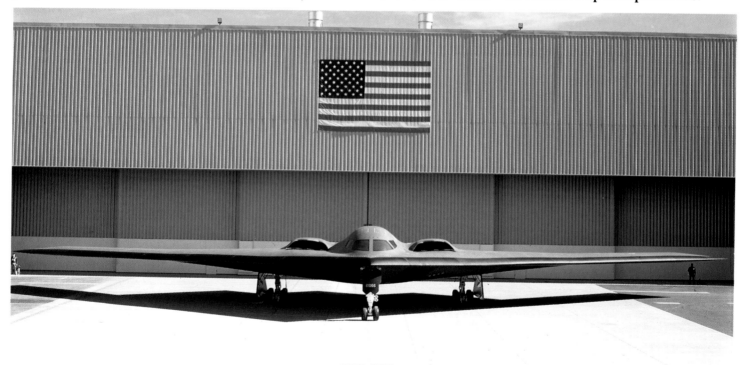

THE military effectiveness of the B–2 depends on its low RCS, and Northrop claims that the B–2 incorporates fourth-generation stealth technology. The claim might raise eyebrows, but the rationale behind the claim is as follows. Typical first-generation stealth technology was the anti-radar coatings applied to the SR–71 Blackbird and B–1B Lancer. Second-generation technology was used on unmanned systems such as the AGM–129 Advanced Cruise Missile (ACM), while third-generation technology flew on the F–117A. On the latter aircraft, however, a penalty had to be paid in the form of increased drag, reduced range and modest payload. Only with the B–2, the Lockheed/General Dynamics YF–22A and the Northrop/McDonnell Douglas YF–23A Advanced Tactical Fighters (ATF) has stealth technology been successfully coupled with high performance.

From Air Vehicle No. 1 (AV–1) onwards, all B–2 aircraft will be built on production tooling, a computer-controlled optical theodolite being used to align the jigs to the required degree of precision. With conventional techniques, this task would take weeks; the theodolite does it in a matter of hours. Wingspan is held to within ± 0.25in (6.3mm), an error of less than one part in 8,000, or 0.012 per cent.

At a meeting of Northrop shareholders held in May 1988, Northrop Chairman Thomas V. Jones described how the tooling "can be adjusted to accuracies of within one thousandth of an inch. The end result is a system that allows every major structural assembly of the B–2, regardless of complexity, to fit together exactly as designed." What he didn't explain was that these exacting tolerances were required to make the aircraft stealthy.

Frontal profile of the B–2 is the simplest possible – two straight, moderately-swept leading-edges which meet at the nose. The trailing-edge, however, takes the form of a massive, five-peak sawtooth made up from 10 straight edges, aligned at one of the same two fixed angles as the leading-edges. The inboard sections are shorter than those further outboard, giving the aircraft a longer-chord centre section similar to that on the F–117A and the 1944 Horten flying wings in Germany.

The reason for this novel planform is that the leading- and trailing-edges

B-2: The Future Revealed

of wings and other aerodynamic surfaces are good radar reflectors. An incoming radar wave arriving at such an edge will behave rather like a light beam striking a reflective surface, or a billiard ball which hits the edge of the table: if it arrives at any angle other than 90deg, it will depart at a similar angle in the opposite direction.

Like the more highly-swept leading-edges of the Lockheed F–117A, the B–2's leading-edges ensure that the main RCS sidelobes in the forward sector are well away from the direction of flight. Radar energy arriving from the

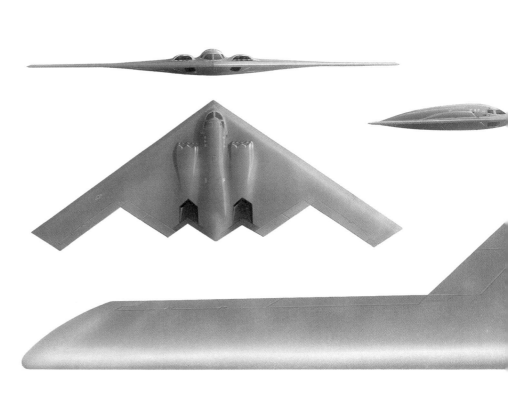

rear hemisphere will tend to be reflected from the trailing-edges in two directions well away from the immediate rear of the aircraft.

This use of surfaces aligned at one of four angles is maintained on smaller features of the aircraft. The leading- and trailing-edges of the main undercarriage doors are angled to match the leading-edges of the wing, as are the corners of the nosewheel door.

On a conventional aircraft, the vertical stabilizer acts as a radar-reflective surface, while any right angle formed by the fin/fuselage junction can trap and reflect radar energy. Elimination of the conventional stabilizer, and small ventral rudders as used on the earlier XB–35 and –49, thus helps reduce RCS. The main gear doors remain

extended while the undercarriage is lowered, an arrangement probably intended to provide vertical area (and thus stability) during low-speed flight.

LEADING LINES

Used on an even smaller scale, fixed angles result in edges having a saw-tooth profile, a feature first used on the Lockheed F–117A. This can be seen on the leading- and trailing-edges of the weapon bays and engine-access panels, as well as on the air intakes.

The planform outlines may be drawn with a ruler, but from all other angles the B–2 is made up of rounded curves whose shape and smoothness are tightly controlled at time of manufacture. Only by strictly maintaining

these complex shapes can the RCS be minimized.

When measuring RCS, radar engineers quote the result in terms of area, usually expressed in square metres (m^2). No official figure has been released for the RCS of the B–2, or for any other US stealth aircraft, but various estimates have appeared in print. Head-on RCS of a B–52 is around $100m^2$, while that of a McDonnell Douglas F–4 Phantom II is around $4m^2$.

In his 1989 book *"Stealth Warplanes"* (published in the USA as *"Stealth"*), the author estimated the RCS of the B–2 as below $0.10m^2$ perhaps as little as $0.05m^2$, but these figures are now known to have been unduly pessimistic: a technical paper published in 1990 by aviation journalist Bill Sweet-

Legend has it that when an ageing Jack Northrop, father of the flying wing, was shown a model of the B-2 in the 1980s, he cried. Nearly 40 years after the first generation of flying wings had been abandoned, his vision of the future had been proved right.

Smooth and blended contours are mandatory on all of the B-2's surfaces, the only sharp lines being on the planform, with all the straight edges aligned at two fixed angles. Despite such novel lines, the B-2 remains extremely fuel-efficient.

The Hidden Warrior

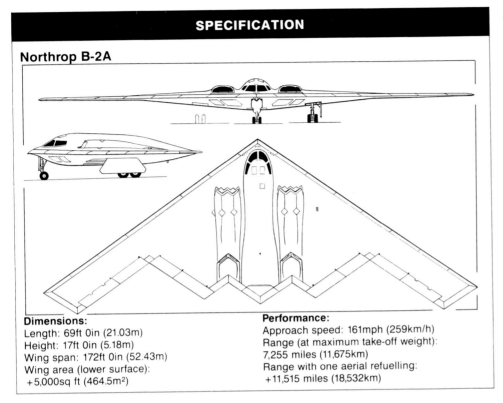

SPECIFICATION

Northrop B-2A

Dimensions:
Length: 69ft 0in (21.03m)
Height: 17ft 0in (5.18m)
Wing span: 172ft 0in (52.43m)
Wing area (lower surface):
+5,000sq ft (464.5m²)

Performance:
Approach speed: 161mph (259km/h)
Range (at maximum take-off weight):
7,255 miles (11,675km)
Range with one aerial refuelling:
+11,515 miles (18,532km)

man revealed that the head-on RCS of the Lockheed A–12 reconnaissance aircraft (forerunner to the Lockheed SR–71 Blackbird) was only 0.015m². For the early-1960s, this was an impressive achievement, but one which was largely wasted. The plumes of efflux from the spy plane's twin J58 turbojets when the aircraft was at high altitude provided massive radar targets, making the aircraft easy to track. Sweetman estimates the RCS of the B–2 to be "about a hundred times smaller than that of the B–1." Assuming that he meant the B–1B, this implies an RCS of around 0.001m².

Even lower figures have appeared in print, but some have bordered on the absurd. In May 1983, the magazine *"Defense Electronics"* quoted an "engineer associated with the [stealth bomber] project" as saying that during target-penetration studies "we're seeing radar cross sections of less than

one-millionth of a square metre. That's incredibly small for a huge airplane". The same figure has since been repeated by other sources.

RCS figures of such magnitude (0.000001m²) are normally associated with tiny insects. Even the humble bee can manage 0.00001m². Were technology to make possible a B–2 with such a small RCS, the radar signature would be drastically increased by the presence of a few dozen squashed bugs on the wing leading-edge!

During a Congressional hearing in July 1990, USAF Chief-of-Staff General Larry Welch was asked if the RCS of the B–2 was most like that of aircraft, birds, or insects. Welch replied that it was "in the insect category". This clearly rules out RCS figures of 0.10m² to 0.01m² (typical values for birds). The RCS of a large insect such as a locust is around 0.001m², a figure which agrees with

the Sweetman estimate quoted earlier.

Radar detection range is not directly proportional to RCS, so the fact that the B–2 may have an RCS one hundred thousandth that of the B–52 does not mean that a radar able to detect a B–52 at a range of 115 miles (185km) could only detect a B–2 at six feet (1.85m). In practice, the hundred-fold RCS reduction between the B–52 and the B–1B would reduce the detection range from the 115 miles (185km) mentioned earlier to around 36 miles (58km). The laws of radar are such that only a massive reduction in RCS will really blunt radar effectiveness. The 0.001m² RCS assumed for the B–2 would carve the range of our hypothetical radar down to just over 3.6 miles (5.8km). In practice, the USAF hopes that the pilots of Soviet interceptors would not be able to detect the B–2 on radar until around the range it could be picked up visually.

RCS SETTING

Having been "designed in" from the start, the RCS will be difficult to vary by any significant amount in any future derivatives of the aircraft. "You must keep in mind that we designed it into the airplane and for a variety of frequencies", says Major General Scofield. "Once you have designed that radar cross section into the airplane, that is probably what it is going to be through its lifetime . . . Radar cross section remains constant throughout the life of the 'plane unless you can find ways to reduce it even further through new technologies."

More than 100,000 RCS images of aircraft models and subsystems had been measured by mid-1990. Once a reliable estimate of RCS was available, this could be used in simulations intended to assess the aircraft's ability to fly combat missions under various operational scenarios. In early-1990, it was revealed that simulations of this nature had predicted that the B–2's ability to penetrate enemy defences was within two per cent of the requirement, but no further details were revealed.

For the eight months after its highly-publicized rollout, the B–2 became the world's best known "hangar queen". Flight testing was due begin in January 1989, but that month came and went with the Northrop bomber still firmly on the ground, apparently plagued by minor technical problems. The first time the aircraft was fully fuelled, several tiny leaks were discovered. One was from a single self-sealing bolt which had been improperly installed; the others were from an area where electrical wiring leading to flight test instrumentation entered a fuel cell. Fuel leaks proved troublesome on many previous US bombers, but on the B–2 they were easily fixed and showed no sign of recurring once the flight test programme finally got under way.

In May 1989, General Bernard Randolph, head of AFSC, finally announced that the aircraft would fly within the next two months. That summer saw an extensive series of taxi tests some of which were carried out on days when the temperature exceeded 38°C (100°F). This allowed Northrop to monitor one potential area of concern – the Lear Astronautics Actuator Remote Terminal (ART). Part of the fly-by-wire system, this had been

RCS	Reduced Radar Range		
	Tracking	Area Search	Volume Search
0.1	0.56	0.32	0.18
0.01	0.32	0.1	0.03
0.001	0.18	0.03	0.006
0.0001	0.1	0.01	0.001

Above: Any reductions in target RCS have a significant effect on radar range, especially when operating against radars that use both area and volume search modes.

Aircraft Size Compared to RCS

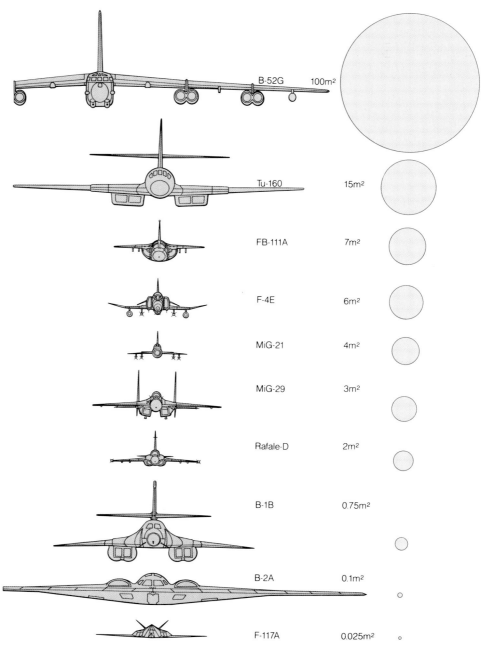

B-52G	100m²
Tu-160	15m²
FB-111A	7m²
F-4E	6m²
MiG-21	4m²
MiG-29	3m²
Rafale-D	2m²
B-1B	0.75m²
B-2A	0.1m²
F-117A	0.025m²

Thanks to stealth technology, an aircraft's RCS is no longer proportional to its physical size, as indicated by the B-2A's position in the table.

The Hidden Warrior

Above: Following its enforced eight-month stay in the hangar, AV–1 was primed and readied for a series of crucial taxi trials along the runway at Palmdale, Ca., during July 1988.

identified as a possible single point of failure, particularly if overheated during taxying by long delays before take-off on a hot day. In practice, the system seem to have performed adequately.

Minor problems continued to delay the programme as technicians prepared the bomber for its maiden flight. A taxi test on 10 July had to be abandoned when the inboard right (No.3) engine ingested a foreign object which had entered its auxiliary inlet door. An attempt to fly the aircraft on 15 July failed when a blocked oil line in one of the engine accessory-drive gearboxes resulted in a low-pressure indication during pre-flight checks.

FIRST FLIGHT

It was not until 17 July 1989 that the aircraft finally flew. Aircrew for the maiden flight were Northrop Chief Test Pilot Bruce Hinds, with director of the B–2 combined test force Colonel Richard S. Crouch acting as copilot. Following a 4,100ft to 5,100ft (1,250m to 1,555m) take-off roll which lasted for 24 seconds, the bomber lifted off of the Palmdale runway, climbing to an altitude of 10,000ft (3,050m). During the 1hr 52min flight, the aircraft reached a top speed of around 217mph (350km/h), while the crew explored handling in pitch, yaw and roll. On arrival at Edwards AFB, it flew an intentional overshoot, then landed without incident.

After landing, Hinds described how the aircraft's flying qualities "closely matched what we had seen in simulation . . . and were better in some respects, particularly in ground effect." The aircraft was nimble, but rock-steady on the approach, he explained. There was no tendency to float in ground effect just before touchdown. On this first flight, the wheels had landed on the runway within 200ft (61m) or so of the aim point. Colonel Crouch summed up the behaviour of the aircraft as being "very well damped directionally, almost dead-beat in pitch, and very well damped in roll."

Under a schedule drawn up long

Below: With thousands of Northrop and USAF personnel in attendance, AV–1 took to the skies for the first time on 17 July 1988. The "flying wing" concept was airborne again.

before the first flight, the aircraft was to spend up to six weeks on the ground undergoing an extensive systems checkout. The second flight was postponed several times, but finally took place on 16 August 1989. This mission

Below: A remarkable and interesting worm's eye view of AV–1, revealing the outline of the bomb bays and the distinctive "sawtooth" configuration of the wing trailing-edge.

saw the undercarriage retracted for the first time, and also the closure of the auxiliary inlets on top of the nacelles. The sortie was to have lasted for 3 to 4 hours, but was cut short when the crew received a low oil-pressure warning from one of the Airframe-Mounted Accessory Drives (AMAD). The aircraft landed after spending only 69 minutes in the air. The AMADs had already proved troublesome during the long pro-

Above: Climbing up and away from the crowds at Palmdale, AV–1 starts what was to be a test flight lasting just under two hours. Note the deflected outboard split-drag rudders.

gramme of taxi trials, and were to cause at least one more of the early test flights to be cut short. Modified replacement units were fitted later that year.

The "flying wing" configuration produces some novel design problems.

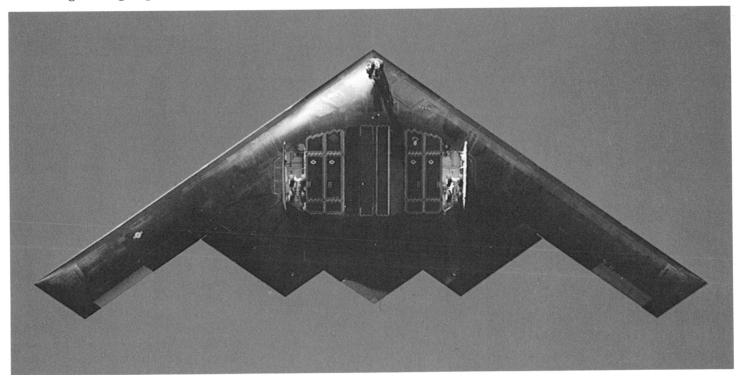

The Hidden Warrior

A conventional aircraft can use wing flaps to increase lift on take-off and landing, but on a flying wing their use creates a nose-down pitching moment. To eliminate this, the other control surfaces must be moved upwards to raise the nose, thus partially countering the effect of the flaps. Design for stealth, and the use of leading-edge slats is effectively ruled out. The wing leading-edge is a significant contributor to RCS, so the addition of slats would almost certainly increase radar reflectivity. The only way to maximize lift is to use the largest possible wing, and the B–2 has a massive wing area of more than 5,000sq ft (465m²).

Control surfaces account for about 15 per cent of the total wing area. These consist of split drag rudders at each wing tip, an elevon on each outboard trailing-edge, plus two more elevons on the next inboard section, and a small moving beaver tail at the aft end of the centrebody beaver tail. The inboard wing elevons are the primary flight controls, operating at all speeds. At low speed, the task of controlling the aircraft is shared by the outboard elevons (which are used only at low speed) and the middle elevons, which are also used at low speed and for gust-alleviation during low-level flight.

Take-off runs begin with the elevons deflected downwards, but these are raised at a pre-selected speed. The reason is not aerodynamic but mechanical: in the event of a hydraulic failure at low speed, the sheer weight of these huge 5ft (1.5m) chord surfaces would cause them to fall open hard against the end stops, perhaps damaging the structure.

The split-drag rudders are used for directional control. During early flights, some observers were puzzled by the fact that these were opened for much of the time. This is because an initial "dead zone" exists beyond which they must be moved for greater effect. On the approach, these surfaces are opened to around 45deg. This makes them as effective as possible, while creating enough drag to allow the engines to be run at a more responsive throttle setting.

All control surfaces are driven by fast actuators powered by the aircraft's 4,000 psi (280 bar) hydraulic systems. Rapid response is essential on a pitch-sensitive configuration such as a flying wing, and the elevons can be moved at up to 100deg/sec.

The aircraft has a quadruplex fly-

Left: As it banks gracefully over the high desert of Southern California, the new bomber's truly massive wing, sharp angles and smooth upper-body blending are clear for all to see.

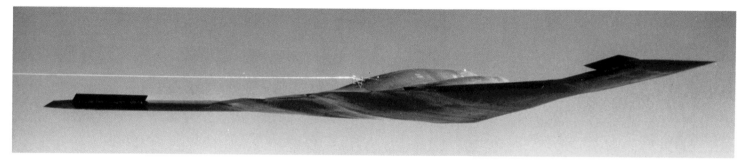

Above: Viewed from a different angle to that shown on the previous page, the B–2 now presents a different set of lines, giving the impression of a far sleeker aircraft.

by-wire system. Probably developed by General Electric, it is similar to that used on late-model F–16 Fighting Falcons, and incorporates a sophisticated stability-augmentation system.

Inlets mounted on the upper wing feed air to the engines buried within the fuselage. A secondary inlet mounted just ahead of the main inlet and offset slightly outboard may serve to remove the turbulent boundary layer, but such precautions are normally taken only on supersonic aircraft. The air drawn in by this secondary inlet is probably ducted down to the engine bay, and used for cooling.

The inlets make a major contribution to the total RCS of many aircraft, and on the B–2 a redesign was apparently needed to get these right, and to solve manufacturing problems associated with their complex shape. The final design combines the complex shape needed for RCS reduction with a certain amount of RAM used to dampen their remaining radar response. When treating hollow (and thus radar-reflective) openings such as inlets and exhausts it is not necessary to line the entire inside walls with RAM, but simply to apply panels of RAM in carefully-selected locations on the inside walls. These show as dark sections within the inlet. The angles of the zig-zag profile of the upper lips of the main intakes and the narrower secondary inlets match those of the wing leading-edges.

POWERPLANT

Two doors on the upper surface of each nacelle are opened when the aircraft is taxiing and flying at low speed. These are auxiliary inlets used to supply extra air to the engines.

The aircraft's General Electric F118-GE-100 turbofan powerplant is a non-afterburning derivative of the F110 fighter engine, and is built on the same production line as the latter. It is 8ft 4½in (2.55m) in length, 3ft 10¾in (1.18m) in maximum diameter, and uses the same core and fan case as the F110. Diameter of the three-stage fan is unchanged, but a new pattern of long-chord fan blade increases the airflow to the engine from 250 to 270lb/sec (113 to 122kg/sec) to around 280lb/sec (127kg/sec). Bypass ratio is reduced from 0.85 to around 0.80, while pressure ratio and dry thrust are boosted. Qualification testing of the powerplant was completed in 1987, and full-scale production of the new engine was initiated in spring 1989.

Below: With everything hanging down and out, AV–1 presents its "dirty" configuration to the camera as it makes its final approach prior to a smooth and uneventful touchdown.

LITTLE is known about the offensive and defensive avionics planned for the B–2. Flight testing of the avionics started in 1986 using a modified Boeing C–135 as a testbed. From early-1987 onwards, this aircraft was used to flight test the Hughes APQ–118 radar. Parts of this radar system were fitted to the first B–2 prototype before its maiden flight, but activation of these was not an early test goal.

The APQ–118 is a high-resolution, low-probability of intercept (LPI) radar system able to detect and classify ground targets. Known to operate in the Ku-band (12–18GHz), it combines conventional search, detection and tracking modes with synthetic-aperature modes customized for penetration and navigation. Dark patches visible under the wing leading-edge on either side of the B–2's nose gear are thought to be for the equipment's conformal antennae. To allow the aircraft to use laser-guided bombs (LGB) when on conventional missions, the USAF ordered the development of an internally-mounted laser designator.

The aircraft's navigation system is believed to be made by Kearfott, with

Honeywell supplying the radar altimeter. Responsibility for the aircraft's EW suite seems to have been split between Raytheon and Sanders Associates, though Northrop's own EW division could also be involved. Testing of the complete EW system will be carried out in a custom-designed anechoic chamber at Edwards AFB, California. Lined with RAM, the wall of the chamber will be able to contain the signals emitted by the B–2 jamming suite, allowing the system to be run at

Above: The unusual surroundings for this B–1B Lancer form the anechoic chamber at Edwards AFB, Ca. The B–2 is set to undergo full-scale testing of its EW suite in this setting.

full power without the risk of the signals being intercepted and analyzed by a hostile intelligence service.

The aircraft will be flown not by a pilot and a weapon-systems operator (WSO) as on the FB–111A, but by two pilots. One will obviously require training in navigation and EW, both when converting to the aircraft, and then to maintain these skills. Having a second pilot will help reduce fatigue on long, intercontinental-range missions, but it remains to be seen just how well this arrangement will work in practice. Will men who have qualified as pilots be prepared to master and refine the additional skills of navigation

Left: As AV–1 picks up speed during its take-off run, sunlight helps to pick out the lines of the APQ–118 radar's conformal antennae housing. A similar housing is on the port side.

and EW, particularly if these cut into piloting duties? A three-man crew might have been a wiser choice.

Each crew member has his own control stick and throttles, plus four multifunction display screens arranged in a "T" configuration – a horizontal row of three, plus another directly below the centre screen. Another centrally-mounted panel incorporating a ninth screen and accessible by both pilots will handle weapon functions.

Significant use is made of automation to reduce crew workload. A master mode switch allows the aircraft and its systems to be configured for take-off, combat and landing. The first mode would carry out pre-flight and other performance checks, then prepare the aircraft and its controls for take-off. Combat setting would deactivate the radios and other potential sources of emission, and prepare the weapons. When landing mode is selected towards the end of the flight, the systems deactivated after take-off would be powered up again, and a checklist worked through to prepare for approach and touchdown.

HANDLING

Early flight trials showed that the aircraft handled well, and Northrop Chief Test Pilot Bruce Hinds has described the B–2 as handling "more like a fighter than a bomber".

Even at a maximum take-off weight of around 370,000lb (167,980kg), wing loading is only 75lb/sq ft (366kg/m^2). By contrast, the maximum wing loading of the B–52H is 122lb/sq ft (595kg/m^2), increasing to 243lb/sq ft (1,186kg/m^2) on the B–1B.

Given this low wing loading, skin friction plays a more important role in aerodynamic drag than lift drag. As a result, take-off speed remains constant irrespective of take-off weight, while cruise speed can be determined by operational needs rather than per-

formance requirements. During airborne refuelling operations, the pilot need make only small adjustments to the throttle as aircraft weight rises – an increase of only a few per cent in engine RPM should be enough to maintain speed.

LIFT-OFF

Take-off roll is relatively short by bomber standards. On the first flight the aircraft is reported to have lifted off at around 205mph (330km/h), but 161mph (260km/h) was rapidly established as the best figure.

Thrust-to-weight ratio at take-off is similar to that of the now retired Avro Vulcan, but the delta-winged British bomber lacked the low drag of the B–2. Chief Test Pilot Bruce Hinds has described the accalaration as exceptional for an aircraft of such size. He described to a summer 1990 meeting of the Society of Experimental Test Pilots how during one early flight: "I put the throttles to just below the maximum continuous thrust and the aircraft just accelerated away. It caught the chase airplanes by surprise."

In aerodynamic terms, the B–2's huge wing is 50 per cent more efficient than that of the B–1B, and approaches that of the Lockheed U–2. Hinds describes the rate of climb as comparable with that of the U–2. "In climb, it is very quick to get up to altitude . . . Even at the Emergency War Order gross weight, the B–2 goes right up to 40,000ft [12,200m]". Combat ceiling is around 50,000ft (15,250m).

The B–2 is almost neutrally stable, and elevon trim is within three degrees of the predicted value. On the B–52, the wing-tips can flex by up to 18ft (5.50m), but the B–2 wing is designed for rigidity, with a deflection of only 18in (46cm) at maximum load. Roll rate is reported to be similar to that of the F–111. Stick forces are light, but early flight tests showed that the

Northrop B-2A
Mission Crew: 2
Powerplant: 4 x 19,000lb st (84.5kN)
F118-GE-110 turbofans
Empty weight: 110,000lb (49,900kg)
Maximum take-off weight:
371,330lb (168,433kg)

Rockwell B-1B Lancer
Mission Crew: 4
Powerplant: 4 x 30,780lb st (136.9kN)
F101-GE-102 augmented turbofans
Empty Weight: 192,000lb (87,090kg)
Maximum take-off weight:
477,000lb (216,365kg)

Boeing B-52G Stratofortress
Mission Crew: 6
Powerplant: 8 x 13,750lb st (61.2kN)
J57-P-43WB turbojets
Empty weight: 195,000lb (88,450kg)
Maximum take-off weight:
+488,000lb (221,350kg)

Meeting The Need

rudder's effectiveness was greater than had been predicted, leading Northrop to consider modifications to the flight-control software.

Drag in level flight is as predicted, as are fuel flows, so range targets should be met. Maximum range at high altitude is more than 6,900 miles (11,100km), rising to more than 11,495 miles (18,500km) with a single air refuelling.

In theory, such a huge wing would give a bumpy ride at low level, but the aircraft is fitted with a gust-alleviation system which uses the mid-span set of elevons and the centrebody beaver-tail to good effect.

On final approach, speed will be around 1.4 times stalling speed, giving a wider margin of safety than on conventional aircraft. As a result of the low drag, the engines are run at close to idle in the final stages of the approach and landing.

Expansion of the flight envelope began on the third sortie on 26 August 1989. This trip aloft lasted for 4hr 36min, and took the aircraft to 345mph (555km/h) and 25,000ft (7,625m).

Following the fifth flight, the aircraft was grounded for modifications, including the replacement of a number of fasteners in critical areas of the structure. Since the aircraft had been assembled, it had been discovered that a significant number of incorrect fasteners had been used during construction. As many as possible were now changed, and plans were drawn up to check the airframe for others during the next period of downtime.

HOOKING UP

Testing restarted on 8 November with a 6hr 5min flight which involved refuelling from a McDonnell Douglas KC–10A Extender aerial tanker. Several hook-ups were made, and 40,000lb (18,160kg) of JP–8 fuel transferred. The next two missions saw further refuelling operations, plus the first in-flight shut-down and restart of the F118 engine.

Under the original schedule for these Block One tests, the aircraft had been expected to fly 15 sorties, accumulating a total of 75 hours in the air.

In practice it flew 16 times, clocking up a total of more than 67 hours of flying time. In the final stages, AV–1 was achieving 50 per cent more flying hours per month than the USAF had expected. No fuel leaks were reported, nor any failures of the onboard fuel and hydraulic systems.

"All the data we are seeing is coming very close to what we had expected to see as a result of the modelling and simulation work done earlier in the programme", Major General Scofield told the magazine *"Defense News"* just before the Block One tests ended. "But we haven't seen anything resembling the problems experienced in previous aircraft programmes." Several months of down time in spring 1990 were needed to incorporate planned modifications, and to prepare the aircraft for Block Two flight testing, which

Below: The relative shortness of the B–2 (as opposed to its wing span) is shown to good effect as it moves in on a KC–10A Extender tanker. A series of in-flight refuelling test hook-ups was initiated in November 1989.

load testing, plus some weapon-separation work, this aircraft is heavily instrumented, and would be difficult to convert to the full production standard at a later date. It has thus been earmarked to remain at Edwards AFB as a test aircraft. By summer 1991, it will have been brought up to a suitable standard for full flight envelope testing.

AV–3 will be the first B–2 to carry a full avionics suite and is tasked with some low-observability work, as well as sharing the avionics and weapon-compatibility testing with AV–4. The next aircraft off the line will be used for climatic testing and some weapons trials, while AV–6 will be used for operational testing and evaluation, low-observable testing and validation of the technical orders which will be used for operational servicing. The goal of the latter exercise is to ensure that when the first operational aircraft enter service, the required maintenance personnel will be trained and in place, complete with documentation and spares to that SAC can begin to task the aircraft with militarily-useful sorties.

would include initial low-observability tests. Intended to demonstrate that the aircraft's RCS was close to the predicted value, these would involve flying at lower altitudes and higher speeds.

LOSSES AND GAINS

The trailing static cone assembly was removed, along with various telemetry antennae, while the external surface was smoothed to production standards. According to some reports, a number of interim components not built to the exact profile needed to minimize RCS were replaced by definitive designs. An autopilot was installed, and more fastener splice plates were added to the wing carry-through box. Doors came in for modification, with steel fasteners replacing aluminium components in the nosewheel unit, and the crew-entry door seals and panels were

Right: The completion and successful flight-testing of AV–2 (foreground) will allow both the USAF and company contractors to progress steadily with testing – if the politicians agree.

strengthened. At the same time, the flight-control software was updated, and the engines were removed for close inspection.

While this work was going on, the second aircraft was being prepared for a first flight in autumn 1990. In its initial form, the first prototype could not cover the entire performance envelope, so that task has been assigned to the second aircraft, AV–2. Tasked with flight envelope expansion and

33

BY the end of the 1990s, the B–2 will be needed as the key component of SAC's bomber fleet. By that time, the combined B–52H and B–1B fleet will number less than 200 aircraft. The Rockwell bomber will be no youngster, with the fleet being around 14 years old; but the B–52s will have passed the 40-year mark. Translated to an earlier era, the latter would be like having Fokker Triplanes in front-line service in the late-1950s, or Spitfires and B–17 Flying Fortresses still operational in the late-1970s!

By the turn of the Century, there can be no question of using the B–52s as penetrating bombers. The USAF withdrew the B-52G from that role in October 1989, and contemporary intelligence estimates suggested that the H-model would have to follow the earlier version into the stand-off role by the mid-1990s. Unless some unforeseen breakthrough in air defence technology were to be achieved by the Soviet Union, the B–1B will remain an effective penetrator until around the year 2005, but would gradually have to be switched to a less well-defended set of targets.

The first B–2 operating base will be Whiteman AFB, Missouri. Named after the first USAAF airman to be shot down in the Second World War, Whiteman is currently the operating base of the 351st Strategic Missile Wing (SMW) and its Minuteman Intercontinental Ballistic Missiles (ICBM). A feature which led to its selection as home for the B–2 was the high-security facilities associated with these ICBM operations.

Whiteman last operated bombers in the mid-1960s, when its B–47s were deactivated. By winter 1988/89, work was underway to repave the runway, install a hydrant fuel distribution system and erect 21 new buildings, including covered alert shelters, covered maintenance spaces for all aircraft not on alert, a mission operations centre, and a combat crew training facility. Extensive use was made of simulators during development of the aircraft, and the task of creating the on-site B–2 training simulator has been assigned to CAE-Link Flight Simulation Corporation.

The aircraft based at Whiteman AFB will be kept under cover at all times when not flying, and the USAF has requested that $450 million be spent on refurbishing 26 existing hangars at the base, and building a total of 64 new hangars plus 32 alert shelters. These figures will be scaled down if the planned reduction of the B–2 force from 132 aircraft to 76 goes ahead.

According to the USAF, the B–2 force needs individual hangars because of "special maintenance and security requirements". Apparently the aircraft will require frequent work on its structure and propulsion system to maintain its low-observable characteristics. The service has denied reports that the B–2 needs to be kept in a climate-controlled hangar; installations of this type would only be needed as repair facilities to allow the "curing" of repairs to composite materials. Purpose-designed hangars will prolong the life of the aircraft's special coating, says the USAF, pointing to the wisdom of equipping these buildings with a fire-fighting system able to protect the B–2 fleet.

Primary B–2 maintenance depot will be the Oklahoma City Air Logistics Center (ALC) at Tinker AFB, Oklahoma, and research into ways of repairing damage to the aircraft have been under way since the early-1980s. Current USAF fighters such as the F–15 Eagle and F–16 Fighting Falcon have metal airframes with little or no composites. US Navy experience with the F/A–18 Hornet and AV–8B Harrier II has given some knowledge

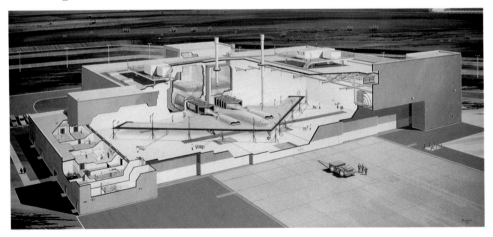

Left: An artistic impression of the B–2 engine testing facility within Northrop's Palmdale facility. The USAF would likewise need such a facility to support B–2 operations.

of composite-repair techniques, but these are intended simply to restore mechanical strength. On the B-2, repair squads must also maintain the aircraft's stealth qualities. In the UK, the RAF has found that metal patches work well on their Harrier GR.5s, but such techniques are out of the question on a stealth aircraft.

Major General Scofield is confident that suitable techniques have been developed for the B-2. "Repair of composite materials is a matter of using the proper kinds of materials, using the proper kinds of glues, and heating them at the right temperature and bonding them together", he told the magazine *"Defense News"* in 1990. "The complexity level depends on the type of damage. It could be as simple as adding additional skin materials . . . or cutting out flawed sections and replacing them."

ON ALERT

SAC hopes that the reliability and maintainability of the B-2 will allow around 55 per cent of the fleet to be maintained on alert at any one time, compared with about 30 per cent for the B-1B. Wheel track of the main gear is 40ft (12.20m), allowing the aircraft to operate from any airfield usable by the Boeing 727.

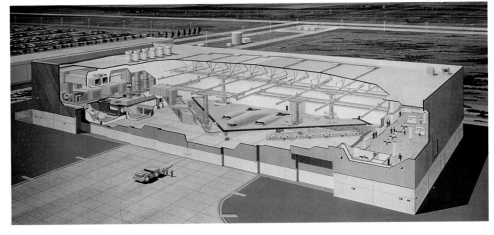

The aircraft's pair of side-by-side weapons bays can carry a maximum ordnance load of 50,000lb (22,700kg). With a payload of 24,000lb (10,896kg) – for example, eight Short Range Attack Missiles (SRAM) and eight 695 to 716lb (315kg to 325kg) B61 100 to 500-Kiloton variable yield nuclear bombs – the B-2 would take off at a weight of 358,000lb (162,532kg), and would carry more than 160,000lb (72,640kg) of internal fuel. Under these conditions, maximum range on a high-altitude mission would be 7,580 miles (12,200km). For a "hi-lo-hi" mission involving 1,150 miles (1,850km) flown at low altitude, range would fall to 5,180 miles (8,335km). A "hi-lo-hi" mission on which the crew were free to

Above: Care and maintenance of the B-2's paintwork will be of vital importance if its capabilities are to be optimized, hence the complex paint shop facility at Palmdale.

chose the best conditions to maximize range (including, presumably, a shorter period at low altitude) could involve a range of up to 6,215 miles (10,000km). Comparable figures for a B-1B fitted with a payload bay tank containing an extra 18,600lb (8,172kg) of fuel would be 6,444 miles (10,370 km), 4,834 miles (7,780km) and 5,468 miles (8,800km) respectively.

Replace the eight B61 bombs with eight of the heavier 2,400lb (1,090kg) B83 1 to 2-Megaton thermonuclear

Northrop B-2A
Mission Crew: 2
Powerplant: 4 x 19,000lb st (84.5kN)
F118-GE-110 turbofans
Empty weight: 110,000lb (49,900kg)
Maximum take-off weight:
371,330lb (168,433kg)

Rockwell B-1B Lancer
Mission Crew: 4
Powerplant: 4 x 30,780lb st (136.9kN)
F101-GE-102 augmented turbofans
Empty Weight: 192,000lb (87,090kg)
Maximum take-off weight:
477,000lb (216,365kg)

Boeing B-52G Stratofortress
Mission Crew: 6
Powerplant: 8 x 13,750lb st (61.2kN)
J57-P-43WB turbojets
Empty weight: 195,000lb (88,450kg)
Maximum take-off weight:
+488,000lb (221,350kg)

Seek And Destroy

weapons, and the payload would rise to 37,300lb (16,934kg). Take-off weight would rise to 371,330lb (168,584kg) given the same fuel load. Maximum range on a high-altitude mission would fall to 7,250 miles (11,668km), while those for a 1,150-mile (1,850km) low-altitude-sector and an optimized "hi-lo-hi" mission would be 5,064 miles (8,150km) and 6,090 miles (9,800km) respectively. Comparable figures for a tank-equipped-B–1B would be 6,330 miles (10,186km), 4,600 miles (7,400km) and 5,386 miles (8,668km) respectively. (A B–1B without the internal tank would return figures between 7 and 10 per cent lower.)

HIDDEN WEAPONS

Ordnance will probably be carried within the weapon bays on an Obedient Bomb Rack (OBR). Being studied by Lucas Western's Flight Structures Division, this would bring computerized "intelligence" to the task of weapon carriage and release, handling the flow of information between the weapons, the aircraft and its crew.

In all these specimen missions, the B–1B would burn 214,600lb (97,428kg) of fuel (about a third more than the B–2) while achieving a shorter range. On intercontinental-range missions, the B–2 will thus require less support from aerial refuelling tankers. On a nuclear strike mission against the Soviet Union, tanker support would be half that needed to replenish the same number of B–1Bs.

Despite the recent relaxation of East-West tensions, the Soviet Union will still be operating modern strategic nuclear systems which only a pene-

Right: Stealth reigns supreme, as a lone B–2 and a trio of F–117As unleash a deadly cargo of ALCMs and a SRAM. For their targets far below, the end is near.

Seek And Destroy

conventional *"Linebacker"*-style bombing role, or as an anti-shipping weapon. The 1970s and 1980s saw US aircraft despatched against Third-World targets such as Hanoi and Tripoli, but the SAM defences of the late-1990s or early-2000s might make such missions hazardous for non-stealthy aircraft.

Committed in support of a US ally in a Third-World conflict, a high-flying B–2 could deliver heavy high-explosive

Below: An F-117A stealth fighter attacks the self-propelled AA guns defending an enemy armour formation (1), while another launches a HARM missile at an SA-8 unit (2) and a third targets resupply routes (3). High above, an Il-76 Mainstay AEW platform falls victim to another F-117A (4).

trating bomber will be able to hunt down and attack. These include the mobile SS–24 and SS–25 ICBMs first deployed in the late-1980s. The B–2 will be able to cruise at high altitude, relying on the fact that its low RCS makes it near-impossible to skin track. From this vantage point, mobile ICBMs and other hard-to-locate targets such as mobile command and control systems, bombers and heavy strike aircraft dispersed to alternate airfields, and even large troop formations, can be detected and engaged.

Hunting down mobile targets will not be the aircraft's primary mission when it first enters service, however. According to General Bernard Randolph, the B–2 "will not be all that particularly good" at attacking relocatable targets, while US Defense Secretary Richard Cheney has explained that when the aircraft first enters service it will not have the full range of sensors needed to locate mobile targets. Location of mobile targets is likely to require a combination of conventional radar, millimetre-wave radar, FLIR, and automatic target-recognition.

To help the US strategic forces locate and engage mobile targets, the

Department of Defence (DoD) requested $20 million in the Fiscal Year 1989 (FY89) Defense Budget for work on improving sensors and target-recognition technologies, plus $15.4 million for longer-term research on advanced sensors. A master plan approved by Defense Secretary Frank Carlucci in spring 1988 was intended to improve US ability to locate and attack mobile targets in the mid-1990s.

EYE PROTECTORS

On the B–1B, the aircrew would fit the canopy with screens incorporating small light-reactive portholes if the risk of being dazzled by nuclear flash seemed likely. These are manufactured by PDA Engineering, and the presence of this company on the published list of B–2 contractors suggests that a similar eyesight-protection measure has been adopted on the Northrop bomber. This could take the form of light-reactive goggles, PDA-developed equipment of this type having been demonstrated for possible use on B–1B.

Like the B–52 and the B–1, the B–2 will have potential uses as a carrier of non-nuclear ordnance, either in the

loads with little danger of interception by fighters or SAMs. Used to deliver "iron" bombs in support of tactical ground operations, they would be as uninterceptable as the *"Arc Light"* strikes in South Vietnam. "In certain [conventional] roles, the ATB will have a formidable capability that could not be matched by any other system", a SAC officer told a 1986 symposium. Tasked with such conventional bombing missions, the aircraft can carry up to 80, 500lb (227kg) bombs.

According to General Randolph: "With just one air refuelling, and operating from just four bases – two US and two overseas – the B–2 could cover any point on the World's land masses on a non-stop radius mission, carrying a full conventional payload. These possibilities could deter a great deal of adventurism." The overseas bases referred to are Diego Garcia in the Indian Ocean, and Guam in the Pacific Ocean.

SEABORNE STEALTH

First evidence that a maritime role was planned for the B–2 came in summer 1990, when Major General Scofield described how the Northrop bomber could perform the maritime-patrol tasks currently assigned to some Harpoon-equipped B–52s. The Boeing bomber is vulnerable to SAM attack, particularly from long-range, heavy, naval SAMS such as the Soviet SA–N–6 Grumble, but the B–2 would be able to cruise at high altitude, maximizing the coverage of its radar. On such missions, its weapon bays would carry nuclear weapons, long-range anti-ship missiles such as Harpoon, or mines.

It may be early to talk of updates, but even before the first B–2 had flown, Northrop was discussing with the Air Force the possibility of "evolutionary improvements" to the aircraft. Planned improvements include the installation of new communications equipment and Boeing SRAM 2 air-to-surface missiles, both scheduled for initial deployment in the mid-1990s.

Stealth over the Battlefield

Below: Roles for the B-2 will include attacks on long-range SAM systems (5), ICBMs (6), airfields (7) and high-value command facilities (8).

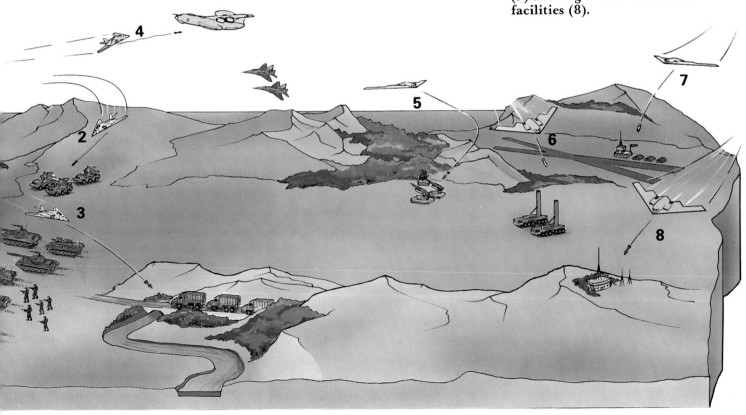

CREATING defences to counter the B–1B Lancer has already forced the Soviet Union to spend six times the sum needed to develop and field the Rockwell bomber, the USAF has claimed. Coping with the B–2 will be even more difficult. From the earliest stages of the B–2 programme, the Pentagon has voiced its continued confidence in the combat survivability of stealth aircraft. Stealth does not make the aircraft completely radar-invisible, but it does dramatically shrink the area coverage of each system. If gaps are not to be left in the defences, large numbers of radars and SAM sites will be needed.

While serving as US Defense Secretary, Caspar Weinberger stated that "To cope with the Advanced Technology Bomber, the Soviets will be forced to make an enormous investment in new defensive systems over a span of many years, while their existing enormous investment becomes rapidly obsolete. The ATB will not only dramatically degrade existing Soviet air defenses, but also those of Moscow's Warsaw Pact allies and Third World client states."

"The defences made obsolete are not limited to the Soviet heartland", says Dr Donald Hicks, Undersecretary of Defense for Research and Engineering. "They include the air defence of Soviet forces in Europe, naval air defence, and air defence of the projection forces of the Soviet Union and its allies . . . If they try to defend against the ATB, the Soviets will need to spend hundreds of billions more. They will be faced with enormously difficult trade-offs among their defensive, strategic offensive and conventional forces."

The Soviet Union does not have the technology needed to create an anti-B–2 defence system, General Welch told the Senate Armed Services Subcommittee in 1989. The cost of creating this technology, then fielding new air defences, would be many times that of the entire B–2 programme.

Welch has denied a 1989 claim by US Congressman John Rowland that the United States had the ability to detect any stealth aircraft entering its airspace, and revealed that the US possessed a *"Red Team"* charged with predicting possible Soviet countermeasures, an effort which has been under way since 1981. This has investigated concepts such as long-wavelength radar, but also novel approaches including one based on the use of cosmic ray detectors.

Coping with stealth aircraft poses similar problems to locating and tracking nuclear submarines – no single technology seems to offer a complete solution. Only by using a range of complementary sensors does the defender have a chance of successfully detecting his elusive quarry.

One widely-described anti-stealth technique involves the use of long-wavelength radar. Equipment such as the Soviet Union's P.14 *Tall King* and P.15 *Flat Face* radar units do not use conventional microwave frequencies, but lower radar frequencies where RAM is less effective.

The wavelengths used by Over The Horizon (OTH) radar can be anything from 33 feet to 330 feet (10m to 100m), so are comparable with or greater than the dimensions of an aircraft. Under such conditions, the amount of signal scattered by a target is independent of target shape. Radar energy would be reflected by the entire airframe, rather than by its individual components.

Left: A derivative of the Soviet's Il–76 transporter, the Mainstay AEW platform can provide a degree of warning of an imminent attack. But can it detect the B–2?

Left: Under the watchful eye of a commanding officer, a Soviet air defence radar crew concentrate on their display screens, searching in vain for that elusive target.

"It's not designed to keep the other guy from knowing that the war has started. What you want to do is counter the things that are going to shoot at you and kill you".

UNDER THREAT?

At the time of the B–2's rollout, press speculation suggested that the new bomber might be vulnerable to radars mounted on orbiting satellites. Such fears seem to have been groundless, for orbiting radars are no longer being considered under the US Air Defense Initiative (ADI) programme.

The reason is not hard to see. Faced with the need to detect a low RCS target, a radar engineer would try to use the most powerful transmitter possible, plus a large antenna which would focus most of this power into a narrow beam aimed directly at the target, and offering a large area to capture the minute amount of energy

The potential anti-stealth capability of OTH radar was publicized during a 1986 defence conference in Canberra, Australia, by Dr. D. H. Sinnott, a senior principal research scientist of the Australian Department of Defence's Research Centre at Salisbury. The Soviet Union *could* use OTH radars to set up an improved anti-bomber surveillance system, Pentagon officials subsequently admitted, but they denied that such OTH coverage would blunt the overall combat effectiveness of the B–2.

The signals from an OTH radar must reach the ionosphere, reflect, then return to the earth's surface, a process which dictates a minimum operating range of around 560 miles (900km). OTH operators would know that a stealth aircraft was approaching, but would be unable to track it at short enough range to alert SAM sites or guide interceptors.

During an *Associated Press* interview in late-1986, a senior US defence official explained the combat role of stealth when opposed to OTH threats.

Bi-Static "Sanctuary" Concept

One possible stealth detector is bi-static radar, a system whose transmitter and receiver are set in different locations.

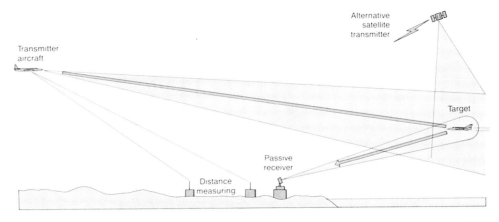

A Dream Fulfilled?

With its greatly reduced radar detection range, the B-2 can pick its way between air defence radar sites, releasing weapons outside the SAM's reduced lethal radius.

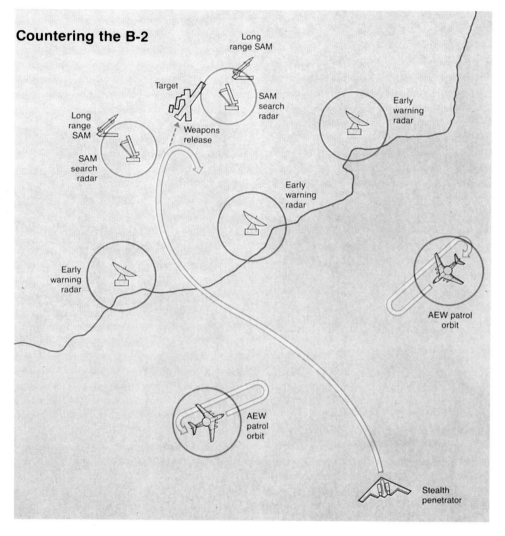

Countering the B-2

Long range SAM

Target

SAM search radar

Long range SAM

SAM search radar

Weapons release

Early warning radar

Early warning radar

Early warning radar

AEW patrol orbit

AEW patrol orbit

Stealth penetrator

reflected from that target. The shorter the distance to the target, the better the chance of receiving an echo.

On any spacecraft, weight and electrical power are limited. Although programmes such as the Rhyolite satellite have shown that large, high-gain, lightweight antennae can be used in orbit, transmitter power would always be modest, while the antenna could never get closer to the target than the

100 miles (161km) or so needed for a long-duration orbit.

Orbiting radars are effective against surface ships and targets whose RCS in square metres is broadly similar in numerical value to vessel displacement in tons, and are used in Soviet ocean-reconnaissance satellites. The technique is unlikely to be of use against low-RCS aircraft targets, however. "You have a real problem with stealthy targets", a

senior DoD official told the magazine "*Flight International*" in 1989. "They are just too far away".

One suggested solution to the problem of detecting and tracking stealth aircraft is to use bistatic radars – systems whose transmitter and receiver are widely separated, giving the latter a chance of intercepting the radar energy scattered in odd directions by features such as the B–2's straight leading-edges. The technique holds some promise, but would be very costly to implement – radar coverage would be be erratic unless large numbers of receiving sites were deployed.

Another suggested counter is impulse radar. This emits short-duration, high-powered pulses of energy spread over a wide band of frequencies. Currently these exist in only a few specialized low-powered forms, and the technology is a long way from being ready for general use. The signal-processing needed to identify the returned echo will be difficult to achieve, but early experiments have convinced the USAF that radars of this type will not be practical as a method of defending against stealth aircraft.

SOARING COSTS

If the B–2 never sees operational service, it is unlikely to be the result of any deficiencies in its stealthiness. Soaring cost may prove its downfall. In the early-1980s, all cost information on the programme was classified, so various unofficial figures emerged. By early-1986 it was being suggested that each B–2 would cost between $500 million and $600 million, and the entire programme would cost up to $79 billion.

That summer, US Defense Secretary Caspar W. Weinberger released cost figures, telling Congress that: "The total estimated cost for research and development and procurement of 132 ATB aircraft is $36.6 billion in 1981 dollars" which "compares favourably to the estimated \$26.5 billion" for the B–1 in 1981 dollars. "Thus the estimated average cost per B–1B is \$265 million dollars, and the cost of the far more capable ATB is \$277 million dollars for each aircraft.

When releasing the first artist's impression of the B–2 in April 1988, the USAF stated that ". . . the Air Force is re-evaluating cost estimates for the programme as a result of current and projected fiscal constraints. When that process is completed later this year, the Air Force will release those updated figures." The costs did indeed rise, and have continued to do so at a steady rate.

As originally planned, the B–2 would probably have been the largest acquisition programme in US military history, Defense Secretary Cheney announced in April 1989, ordering that the Pentagon's Defense Acquisition Board review the entire programme.

As part of a series of cuts intended to trim the FY90 Defense Budget by \$10 billion, President Bush decided early in 1989 to slip the B–2 programme by at least one year, cutting \$855 million in FY90 and a further \$3.2 billion in FY91.

By the end of 1989, it was becoming obvious that the planned 132–aircraft fleet would never be built. During that year, Congress asked the USAF to report on the implications of deploying three or even two Bomb Wings instead of the planned four. Such a move would reduce the fleet size to 90 to 100 or 60 to 70 aircraft respectively.

By May 1990, a final total of 76 seemed likely, with Cheney telling Congress that this could be done thanks to "the changing face of Europe and promising trends in the Soviet Union." The number of aircraft to be bought in FY91 would be reduced from five to two, so that more testing could be completed before the production rate built up. Instead of climbing to

more than 20 aircraft per year in the mid-1990s, the production rate would be held down to between 10 and 12. This would save around \$14.4 billion, while still providing enough aircraft to field two Bomb Wings.

SAFETY IN NUMBERS

The USAF fought a rearguard action against the proposed reduction in numbers, claiming that the need for 132 aircraft had been verified by a 1989 SAC study. Defending the B–2, the service pointed out that its projected delivery accuracy, and the yield of its nuclear bombs, made this the most

effective weapon for use against strongly-hardened targets such as missile silos and heavily-fortified command and control bunkers.

Without the full force, the USAF argued, by the late-1990s the high-priority, hard-to-destroy targets earmarked for assignment to aircraft 77 to 132 would have to be reassigned to other, less accurate delivery systems such as the Peacekeeper and Trident

Below: How the "boomer" aboard an aerial tanker views the unique and menacing outline of the B–2, as it sates its thirst via the telescopic flying boom and flush receptacle.

A Dream Fulfilled?

II ballistic missiles, and the new AGM–129 Advanced Cruise Missile. Launched against hardened targets, these would be only 80 per cent as effective as the B–2. Some civil analysts disagreed, claiming that uncertainties associated with any wartime operations would be greater than the 20 per cent shortfall being discussed by the USAF.

By summer 1990, total cost of the revised 76-aircraft programme was estimated at $61 billion, according to Cheney. Programme cost per aircraft would have been $337 million per aircraft in 1981 dollars, but splitting the development costs over a fleet half the planned size had inflated this figure to $495 million. This corresponded to $752 million in 1990 dollars, or $814 million in mid-1990s dollars.

Unit flyaway cost – the price per aircraft less that aircraft's share of the development costs – was estimated at $265 million in 1981 dollars, $417 million in 1990 dollars, and $492 million in mid-1990s dollars. According to the USAF, annual operating costs for a B–2 Bomb Wing are expected to be similar to those of a B–52G Bomb Wing. Given the sophistication of the newer aircraft, spares will be much more costly, while its stealth characteristics will make it more expensive to maintain; but this will be partially offset by some reductions in manpower levels.

BOMBER BUDGETS

Despite its high cost, production of the B–2 would consume a smaller proportion of the estimated US Defense Budget than the B–52 or B–1B did in their day. Between 1952 and 1961, the B–52 accounted for an average of 1.4 per cent of the Budget, while the B–1B consumed around 1.6 per cent in the early- to mid-1980s.

Thirty years ago, the USAF could buy a B–52G for $7.69 million, or a B–58A for $12.44 million. Allowing a factor of 30 for the effects of three decades of inflation suggests that in real terms, the unit flyaway cost of a B–2 is about three times that of the aircraft it will replace. That looks like good value for money to this author, but many US Congressmen don't share that view. A 76-aircraft fleet might be smaller than USAF planners would like, but it is also bigger than some US politicians would like to see authorized and funded.

By summer 1990, one faction in the US Congress had proposed a cutback to only 15 operational bombers; a move which would eliminate the planned annual production cost of between $7 billion to $8 billion in the early- to mid-1990s. Once the cost of research and development had been divided amongst such a small fleet, along with cancellation costs for unbuilt aircraft, the final price-tag for each B–2 would rise to around $2,400

million. By June 1990, opponents of the programme in the House of Representatives were drawing up a proposed B–2 Termination Bill.

UNCERTAIN FUTURE

Northrop was by then under contract to build eight FSD aircraft, two structural test airframes and five production aircraft. Long-lead funding for five more had been agreed, and a contract for these was under negotiation. The FSD aircraft were more than 75 per cent complete, and due to join the test fleet over the next twelve months, while the initial production aircraft were already 50 per cent complete. Experience on these first 11 aircraft has shown a decline in the number of manufacturing hours needed for each aircraft, but the GAO reported in early-1990 that the reduction was less than had been predicted by the USAF. Northrop hopes that, pound for

pound (or kilogram for kilogram), the B–2 will eventually require no more manufacturing man-hours than a Boeing 757 airliner.

It all sounds reminiscent of the stop-go history of the XB–70 and B–1. Given the catalogue of bomber-procurement blunders which date back some forty years, it's hard to believe that a nation now racked with defence indecision managed in the 1950s to build B–47E Stratojets at a peak rate of more than 400 a year, and B–52 Stratofortresses at a peak rate of more than 100 a year.

Perhaps Congress should decide not to spend another nickle on new bombers, or any other new military aircraft, until Republicans and Democrats in both Houses of the US Congress are able to sit down together and agree that the B–2 programme is worth supporting through the several decades it will take to complete. If a small nation like Sweden can forge such

political agreements, and go on to develop and deploy in quantity fine warplanes such as the Saab-Scania Draken and Viggen, perhaps the West's largest democracy ought to do likewise.

According to a USAF paper written in 1990, "stealth technology is among the most significant military technologies to appear since the advent of radar and the atomic bomb – and one in which the United States enjoys an unprecedented lead." Unless the B–2's supporters can win the day in Congress, that lead could be virtually thrown away, with little to show for a programme which has already cost more than $20 billion.

Below: A truly awesome creature in a cloak of grey – and grey is the best way to describe the future of this controversial bomber. Will it enter operational service, or will it be killed off by the politicians?